LARRY D. JAMES

# "Your new boss looks like this"

*AuthorHouse*™
*1663 Liberty Drive*
*Bloomington, IN 47403*
*www.authorhouse.com*
*Phone: 1-800-839-8640*

*First published by AuthorHouse 01/08/2011*

*ISBN: 978-1-4520-9868-5 (sc)*
*ISBN: 978-1-4520-9843-2 (ebook)*

*Library of Congress Control Number: 2010919015*

*Printed in the United States of America*

*This book is printed on acid-free paper.*

*Certain stock imagery* © *Thinkstock.*

This book is dedicated to my mother Robbie whom I Love very much, my step father Seth who played a very important roll in my life, God rest his soul, along with my Brothers, my Sister, both my children Jeffery and LaNeetra, and all 5 of my beautiful grand children. Thanks for all your support and motivation.

# Table of Contents

# Chapter One - No more Job Security

Never before has job security been so difficult to attain or maintain. Many times we are not even able to qualify for a position that has the benefits such as health, dental, vision and the like. So what exactly has happened to our system that no longer allows us to work for twenty, twenty five, or even thirty years and retire with dignity and respect? Well some say its lack of opportunity, others say it's because people are living longer and the benefits are running out, and still others say it's because of technology. I agree with all of the above and probably several others, however now is the time to actually begin to think in terms of you owning your own business. Ok, now after realizing that the business of handling your business has changed I want to take you on a short journey so that you can understand just how simple and easy it is to start your new business. Since computers have changed the way business is done in the new millinumn the way you start, maintain, and grow your business has changed also. In the past you would finish high school, go to college, after four years in your chosen field graduate, get a job in corporate America get two to five years experience and transition into owning your own company. Today your outline looks more like this, graduate high school, maybe go to college for one or two years and quit only to get a job that pays just enough to keep you there, and consequently you do just enough not get fired.

Or you may finish high school join the military go in for four to six years acquire a skill that you can use in the civilian world if you are able to decide what skill you want to learn before you join. Many times when a young person decides to serve their country and perform their military duties they will enlist on what's called an open contract and by doing that they are actually placed where they are needed instead of where they would want to learn the skill for the civilian world. I know this because I was in the Marines, right out of high school and I enlisted not knowing anything about how the system worked and was placed in Infantry. Fortunately after a year I was able to move into the supply field but the opportunities available as a career after my three years were somewhat limited. The beauty of technology in the 2000's is it eliminates so many of the tangibles of the past, things like you no longer have to physically go to a location to pay your bills, you no longer have to go to the location to apply for a job, you don't even have to attend a university any more you can do all those things and more online. Now one of the down sides of those benefits are they eliminate jobs. And as you can imagine, that's a major downside. So what does that cause us as employees to do, it causes us to become more creative. Never before has it been easier to reach so many people so quickly and because of that we are able to start and run our own online business, and all from the comfort of your own home.

One of the caveats involved in owning your own business is the learning curve. When you work for someone else they handle all the details all you have to do is show up and perform your job and go home. When you own your own business you have to constantly learn in order to grow. If you don't want to learn owning your own business is probably something that doesn't interest you because you will be required to wear several different hats. But having said that, it will become imperative that you consider some type of home based business even if only on a part time basis. The economy has begun to dictate that for sure you cannot rely on a job for 20 to 30 years anymore. And for that reason alone at some point you will probably need to supplement your income and your choices are going to be very limited because of the number of people out of work.

There are three very significant things I stay focused on in life and they are the Mind, Body, and the Spirit. I am a person who also believes equally in Balance, meaning you can do almost anything you like as long as you are able to maintain balance, and not over do anything. The mind, body, and spirit should be continuously worked on or added to. I mean everyday of our lives we should be adding to those three. And because we are not perfect we are going to make mistakes, being able to accept responsibility for those mistakes and moving on allows for the growth that comes with the experience.

The vision involved within me deciding to write this book was because of my interest in online marketing along with today's unemployment rate. I see and hear story after story of people who have all of a sudden gone from making 100K plus per year to having to go to food pantries to get food and sanitation products. I see people who have not been able to find a job in 12, 18, even 24months and more. Then there are those of course who don't have the skills or the education to compete in being able to get a job that will allow them to take care of their families. So consequently, I have been lead to attempt to open the eyes and perhaps some doors for not just the have's that no longer have, but the never have had's as well. One of the true's of the world is no one person is better than another so with that spirit in mind I want to incorporate some of what's known as specialized knowledge to a large group of people about being able to successfully start and run their own home based business. And I will do it with accurate and valid information that people on all levels can understand and apply to their own purpose or what we call reason for being here, because when you are able to work in your true purpose it's not work it's simply living your purpose.

The title of this book was inspired by a conscious realization that today; one not only needs to become computer literate, but also needs to learn how to generate another type of income based not so much on working for someone else as working for themselves. We all have skills, abilities, and things that we really enjoy doing. And if you are able to identify what those are for you, and can be shown a way to generate a second income on a part time basis simply by learning and applying a few new things, I truly believe people will want to learn and begin to think outside the box for a better way for themselves and their families. Never before has information been so easy to acquire and much of it is free to access. Not long ago I made a video called No Money Required that spoke about when you don't have money that is the Best time to learn because you have plenty of free time, and no money to distract you because when you have money you spend money that takes away from your focus. Now the Beauty of learning while your resources are limited is it allows you to connect more with the mind, body, and spirit we spoke about earlier. Along with preparing you for the actual receiving of the money or income that you begin to get, because many times money can be corruptible if you're either not prepared or the amount is more than you are accustom to having.

One of the things that I will share with my readers is Terms that are very important to become more literate with computers. Now as I indicated there will be a bit of learning involved to successfully get your online business up and running, so learn those terms and follow the path that I will be setting up for you and your results will be positive for the growth of your business. Keep in mind that success is a process, and just like yesterday you didn't know you wanted to have an online business, and today you do, will require you to grow in at least one area and probably many areas that you didn't have to yesterday. One of the things that seem to help me when I am required to learn something new is I want to be able to teach it, because at that point I know that I know it. A little Tip: "The computer is the vehicle to the success of your business from this point on". Now having said that, it's not difficult to learn and understand when introduced correctly. Just keep in mind that when you are able to practice what you've learned practice because repetition is a way we learn.

When you are deciding on an online business one of the major things that you should consider is the fact that you will be spending and enormous amount of time doing what it is you select so make certain that it's what you enjoy. Now when I say you, I mean you, not your mother, wife, father, teacher, preacher, anyone but you because at the end of the day you will be able to look yourself in the mirror and say well I can't wait until tomorrow to get back to it. I have known people who spend their entire life doing what we call trying to live up to someone else's expectations, and we all know that's not only impossible, but it's not the way we were designed. We were designed to live our life according to the special gifts that the Lord we pray to has given us. And by doing so we are living our lives in line with our purpose.

Once you have selected your business type, next you will want to begin thinking about how you want to market your product or information. There are several different ways to let people know what you are offering. And with the internet being so effective in reaching people all over the world it has never been easier to connect. A few of the quicker ways to market online is through the classifieds, through your own website, your blog, several different social media site's such as face book, twitter, linked-in, and there are many many more.. You even have access to market online via audio, or video the resources are really unlimited. Keep in mind that the process involved to market online requires a few skills that you don't have at this point, but I will guide you every step of the way. Another reason that I felt compelled to write this book was that I see more and more people in the forty to fifty range who really know very little about computer's, and the jobs they work have absolutely no type of retirement plan. And they truly have no idea what they would do if they were to loose that position they call a job. The second reason was that the economy is in such terrible shape right now and is suppose to be that way for at least the next few years. The unemployment rate is over the top, and the jobs that are available are low paying and have very few benefits. Along with that the high school graduation rate is constantly going down which means that the people who don't have a diploma can't even compete for the normal jobs. That fact alone leads many in that age range to believe that they can't become viable and productive citizens, which is far from the truth. Thanks to the internet and its reach YOU can NOW start your very on cash producing online business, and all that's required is a computer, and a little specialized knowledge to start. Of course you will want to invest in your business as you begin to make money. But by far the biggest investment for your success will be you gaining the few skills required to maneuver around the World Wide Web.

On the internet there are literally hundreds and even thousands of companies to join and become an affiliate with, but before you decide on one there are a few things to consider before joining, and I will go into more detail later but for now just be mindful that you'll want to ask yourself whether the management is experienced in building their own network organization. Many people join companies as affiliates and do everything they are required to do but still don't make any money or they may make 50 or 100 dollars per month, which in this or any other business is not acceptable if you are setting up your system to retire one day. Just a few tips to use when thinking about becoming an affiliate: 1. Do a Google search for the owners of the company, 2. In the Policy and Procedures section as you are reading it, and you should read it; look for things like "Termination, with or without cause" or "Unreasonable". 3. Always ask yourself whether or not the contract protects you or the company. Now that's just a few of the things you should do in the beginning, but a few tips that indicate for SURE that you are involved in a SCAM is: If it's a Cash Only business, or if you can buy a position at the Top, these are 100% scams so be aware and if you are in one you should get out as soon as possible.

Another indicator to ponder is has the company passed the two year time line most start up companies fail within. One of the reasons you want to consider this is because involved with start ups are what's known as growing pains and that means things will come up that the company perhaps didn't expect and they will have to make adjustments when they arise. Did you know that 97to 99% of companies don't last two years? What about, did you know that it's a bad idea to join a company that has passed it's "momentum phase" and have become familiar to most people. When companies use the phrase "get in on the ground floor" their really saying bring all your skills, your money, your contacts, etc. And help us grow our company and if you are able to make a few dollars along the way, its ok if not that's ok to. Since they don't have a track record that will indicate success and if they are affiliated with a publically traded company their first allegiance is to their investors, not you.

There are a number of terms someone interested in the internet marketing business should become familiar with. Knowing the rules of how things are done will shorten your journey in understanding how to benefit from them. Just like you need to know terms, you will also need to work on acquiring certain skills such as, copy and paste, upload, download, just to name a few. And some of the terms would be, server, host, client, browser, and on and on, now don't get discouraged because of all the things necessary to effectively get the job done, it all comes together fairly quickly after you begin. Another Tip, I want to leave with you in regards to learning this process is: Success leaves clues and you would be shocked at how many people begin their systems just like someone else, almost to the point of duplication. As long as you are not violation any infringement rights you are ok. Always remember there will be people who will come behind you, and the same thing you will learn they to will have to learn as well, very few changes will be necessary for them to succeed because the real change comes from within yourself and not the system.

One of the nice things about marketing online or off line is you can be an expert in what ever the field you select. That means once you have learned a particular topic or subject when you introduce yourself to the marketing world you can be the Coach, Mentor, Guru, and so on. All this is possible because you are simply teaching others how to do what it is you have learned, and for that reason you have full rein

# Chapter Two - Your Money and your Time

*I made a few mistakes (on purpose) find them and go to CashfromSocialMedia.com for you new business opportunity.*

I now want to enlighten you a bit about the financial commitment involved in marketing online. As with any other business you will be required to invest into your company, but the fact is the cost is absolutely on the low end of the spectrum. To give you an example I market using videos also and the cost of my very first camcorder cost about 150.00 and I still use it today, I have others now, but I have been able to make well over 100 videos using that camcorder and upload them to different video sites as well as my websites and blogs. You don't need batteries just plug it into your computer and it charges itself, and the instructions are super simple, just the way I like.

Ok, now the hard part is over, you have decided you are going to start a home based business of your very own; do you quit your job yet? Do you go and buy all new equipment? Do you pay hundreds on advertising, absolutely not? Remember this, when a individual starts a home based business, chances are good that they will have to do some type of job and work on their business on a part time basis. One of the reasons for this is there is a learning curve that has to be filled, there's an old saying that says, the more money you have the less knowledge you need and the more knowledge you have the less money you need. So having said that, you will need to spend some time increasing your knowledge, not much and it will be fun because you are working on you. And you don't want to simply quit your job at least until you have doubled your income for six months, or have duplicated your income for a year.

One of the ways I suggest for you to work on your business is to designate time out of your schedule that you can work within your business. Two hours per day four days per week, Three hours per day three days per week, One hour per day, five days per week, it really doesn't matter, what matters is that you are consistent. My advice to beginners is also not to try and do too much to fast or to learn everything at once, and the reason I advise that is to avoid burnout. Although you are doing something that you enjoy and you know it's your business, you still have to try and stay as balanced as possible. You have to remember that there is only 24 hours in each day and you want to try and be your best each and every day which requires you to get your rest, have some you time, if you have a family you will definitely need to spend time with them and on and on. As your understanding of the ins and outs of your business become more familiar to you, you will begin to free up some time, because at some point some your business duties can be outsourced. Another of my recommendations is that initially you do as much of the work as possible so that you know exactly what's taking place. I want to go into a little about possibly the best way to market you online and that's video marketing. One of the keys that you will want to focus on when marketing is the term BRANDING, that's what makes you stand out, it's the song associated with you, it's the logo that when someone see's it they know it's you, and it's the statement that you always use at the end of every video. Well you get the idea of just how important it is so I will start by saying it's literally one, two, three, to learn the process involved. Think about this for a moment, you shoot the video perhaps one to two minutes long, you play it back and decide that you like it. You insert the camcorder's usb into your computer's usb port, after doing that the computer recognizes it and you simply save it to your desktop or document, or any place you like. After you have completed uploading the video all you have to do is go to YouTube or any other video site or even perhaps your website or blog and go to your video page upload the video from your desktop or where ever you have it saved and include a few things like the title, a brief description, a few tags, and you are done. That's it you look like a genius. Now keep in mind that this process requires you to learn a few terms, along with a few techniques, but once your business is up and producing cash the payoff will be well worth it. There are several different types of camcorders that you can use but for beginners I like to recommend the Flip Mino camcorder, simply because of the simplicity of the entire recorder, along with the fact that they are under $150.00. And everything that you will need comes with it except a tripod and for that I recommend the Gorilla Tripod, it's less than $50.00 and they work great together. As an online marketer it's always a good idea to focus on being able to give back. There are several reasons for that, but from an internet perspective the first direction for the marketer should be to give value. Many times when someone is introduced to internet marketing they think that their first move should be to show the products or information to their prospective customers. WRONG!! The online marketing family doesn't operate that way; remember everyone online is not looking to spend money. And there's a mindset called the 7 points of contact. More often than not the first time someone is introduced to your product, or whatever it is that you are marketing they are not going to buy. And more puzzling than that many will feel as if they are being forced or pushed into something that they are not interested in. So you may ask yourself how do I get my product in front of the possible customer. That's easy the absolute best way is to offer value to the possible customer, in the form of a FREE newsletter, audio, video, eBook and the list goes on and on. To bring the concept closer and clearer, the 7 points of contact I mentioned earlier could be something like this: the first contact may be a quote that you post on one of the media sites, such as face book, twitter, or linked-in just to name a few. Often someone will like the post and respond, at that point that can be considered 1 point. Another point would be if you have made a video and uploaded it to YouTube or any of the other video sites and someone clicks on it that's another contact. You may like to write, and decide to write articles and people can read your article and YES that is also another point of contact. As you can see there's an unlimited number of ways to contact a customer, however I will again reiterate you are NOT selling at this point you are simply giving something of value. The selling comes later.

What I would like to describe to you now is what's called a SALES FUNNEL. Imagine for a moment the shape of a funnel, that's correct it's wide at the TOP and narrow at the BOTTOM. At the very top we have several prospects; however they are not qualified just yet. They may be willing to purchase your product: but they need more information to determine if what you are offering is of interest to them. At this point there are a number of what if's involved in the mind of the prospect, things like, maybe they can't afford your prices, or perhaps they can do without your product right now. The more you connect with these prospects, the easier it will become for you to determine whether they will convert to a customer. Remember every time you make a contact with the prospect it will get easier to understand any resistance they may have and learn how to overcome them. Now as you are working your way down the funnel two things begin to happen: your prospects begin to decrease in number, and the remaining prospects become better qualified. Finally, once your prospect reaches the bottom of the funnel they actually become your customer, that means they pay for your products, and prepare to accept delivery. SUCCESS!!! But it get's even better once you have gotten your prospect from the top to the bottom you don't just want the one sell once, you will want to sell to them again and again. One technique to accomplish this is would be to ask them to create an account or opt-in for future email communications. By doing so you actually establish a relationship with your customer and can send out regularly timed emails with value intense content. Auto responders are the tool of choice when setting up a system to automate communication. Also EVERYONE who signs up with your site should receive an email in response, and if they purchase a product your auto responder can send a thank you message. One of the beauties of the sales funnel is that you are actually able to watch the prospect move down the funnel with every point of contact until they finally purchase your product. Now that you have processed five or ten prospects through your funnel and you are sure that everything works properly, your next step is to simply increase the number of prospects that you send to the top of the funnel. Think of the funnel as a qualifier, while at the top your prospects are window shopping, after they receive more material of value they move down to the next level, and finally after you have introduced to the prospect that you are a person of value and can be trusted they are in turn more likely to not only buy from you, but feel good enough about buying that they will recommend you.

Here I will to talk with you a little while about the necessary mind shift that must take place in order for you to go from employee to employer. Many times you never think along those lines simply because you have always viewed yourself as working for someone else. In today's life and times we are being forced to view other avenues not only for success but also to maintain from day to day. As I write this book today on the 5o'clock news the city of Dallas gave notices to some 400 city employees that they would be laid off as of September 30th. Many of those workers have been on the job for ten or fifteen years, and most have very few skills other than what they have done on that job. Now they are being thrust into the mindset of what do I do now, and what can I do? How will I survive, where will I get another job, and the list of what's going on. More often than ever before the answer is I DON'T KNOW. Now let's say you have been learning a skill on the side or have began a small business and were only doing it part time at this point you would have options, simply because you actually have another skill that you can do or even better still you have a small business that you can now devote full time to getting it up and running. Just because one stream of income dries up and in today's market you can almost count on that happening, simply because of owners having to adjust to the economic times. So what should you be thinking when you want to have your own business, first you need to understand that this shift is not at all like the mind of a employee. Things will have to happen and they will be overseen by you, yes you. The completion of all the necessary tasks will be either done by you or overseen after it's done by you. Records will need to be kept, accounts paid, inventory maintained, and the list goes on and on. And although you will be very, very busy you must constantly increase your knowledge about the business you're in. Remember you are no longer the employee but, the employer.

Answer this question for me if you would, have you been feeling like we are living in an era of unprecedented change? Have you been experiencing some extreme challenges in your life? Exactly, and many others are as well, let me ask you how are you coping with the change? Are you ready to make a complete change in what you have been doing? Well history has always dictated that in some of the worst of times some of the best and most creative opportunities arise. Perhaps now is the time to revisit what you really want in your life and take action like you never have before? Maybe your values have shifted and now you want to focus more on what really matters to you. Regardless of the reason the opportunities are here you only need to decide and begin, start to use one percent of one hundred other people's effort instead of one hundred percent of your own.

I want to take this time to personally thank you for choosing to view my very first book. The mission of this book is simply to introduce to you an opportunity for you to evaluate your position in life, right where you are. Also to open a door to the world of self employment in the new millinumn. The world of the old brick and mortar as a start up is all but gone. In today's start up business all you need is a computer, and just a small amount of knowledge about setting up certain specific tools. Whether you are working full time, part time, or even unemployed if you are looking for a better way of life, more freedom to be with your family, more cash to do some of the things that you always wanted but never had the money to do, NOW is the perfect time. The fact that you are looking at this book is evidence that you want to change the course of your life. You have heard all the stories of how this person went from a homeless situation to where they were making six or even a seven figure income in twelve months or less. Well I am not going to tell you that you will be doing that here, not that you won't, but what I am interested in teaching here is the process involved to get to that point. There will be terms that I will cover that right now you are probably not familiar with, or possibly have never heard of. Learning and understanding exactly why you need them, and what they do, will increase your ability to better benefit from setting your system in place. This process will also require you to make a shift in the way you think about your free time, because of the learning curve. With significant growth come significant sacrifices. One of the main reasons for the need for your mental shift in your thinking is you will begin to spend large amounts of time alone. Remember building this business is your dream, your passion, and your decision to make it successful. And I suggest that while spending the necessary time you need to learn, that you not forget the really important things in your life. These are things like your family, your friends, your health, your religion, and so on. Because computers are the new storefront and if you have a job you have to go and work and while you're there for eight hours per day and possibly one or two hours overtime you are spending all that time away from the things that are important to you. Now add a side business that you are setting up online and you may find yourself spending two, three, or even more hours per day learning and positioning your home based business to be able to generate the income you desire. So always remember to balance the new things in your experience along with the old.

My story and my journey has been one of finding myself through a process of life experiences along with business experiences, and what I like to call learning experiences. At the age of seventeen I wanted to become a psychiatrist, I knew my parents couldn't afford to send me to college so I decided to join the army and get the GI benefit to go to college. But before I signed up a friend of mine said that he and a couple of other guys were going to the Marines on the buddy system which meant they would all stay together through boot camp and I should join them. And at the time I really didn't see much difference in the branches and my motivation was not to stay for a career I only wanted to get the benefits so I agreed. I graduated high school on May 28th and June 30th I was standing on the footprints at MCRD in San Diego California. Wow, what an experience, I completed my three year commitment on active duty, received an honorable discharge, moved back to Oklahoma and started my college career. Since I had been in the military I was able to get a job at an Air Force base, I worked full time and went to school full time. Needless to say I was on track, and things were falling in place just as I had planned. I went to a Junior College first, received an Associate in Science in two years. Next step was to transfer to a University which I did and after the first full year there I got caught up in what I call the fast life, and I was no longer able to maintain my grades, at that point I was making real good money and I made a decision to change my major to business, because for me the classes weren't as difficult or time consuming. However I was very much into myself at that time and before long I had made another decision, which was to quit school, after all it was 1979 and I was making over $40.000 per year without another degree. Now one of my major motivations for wanting to quit school was I wanted to move for Oklahoma to Dallas, I was in Dallas every weekend for about 4 months, trying to get my job transferred but there was never any openings. So what I decided to do was resign, sell everything I own except my car and clothes and move to Dallas and in 1984 I did. I didn't really know anyone except a friend that let me stay with her for six months until I found a job. Now I did have money because I closed all my accounts. Within two months I had a job and within four months I had an apt and my new life was taking off.

The reason I'm telling you this is because many people have opportunities that present themselves and when they do, rather than seize the moment they make excuses and remain in what we call a safe zone. Because I could have stayed in Oklahoma and continued working I enjoyed my job, but my location was what I need to change for me to grow. My atmosphere if you will. From that point I never looked back and never regretted the move. Now I don't want to get off the path of this book to far however every now and again it's good for us to see real world experiences that relate to our situation. When deciding to write this book another thought that I incorporated was through whose eyes I wanted the perspective to come from. In other words if you were reading this book for the first time why did you select this particular book? Was it the title, the art work, the photo, or something else? And for me I wanted to reach that person who wants to really become an entrepreneur. First there are millions of books, magazines, tapes, and on and on about that subject, but my experience has always been that where ever you are on your journey to your idea of success and freedom there are thousands if not hundreds of thousands of people exactly right where you are. And more profound than that, is that, there's always more coming every day. So you may ask yourself if the entrepreneurial side of life is so great why is it so elusive to so many? That question has many reasons and my thought on that is, the individual who wants to become self employed, a business owner, CEO of their own company or either way you want to title it must be willing to learn continuously, and apply the things he or she has learned. While doing your business you will make mistakes you only need to learn from those mistakes make the corrections and go on. Now I want to share something about the business world that I have learned along my journey, this is very, very important to remember. And it's simply this, many times the business that makes you the most money or gives you the most recognition, or even becomes your brand and your major business may not the business you began with. Let me give you an example: when I started speaking my very first paid speaking engagement paid me seventy five dollars to speak one hour about wholesaling real estate. At that time I thought WOW I'm on my way, all I need to do is keep getting booked to speak and I can eventually increase my rates and before long I will be a successful speaker and speak all over the country. Then after studying how speakers really make money it was like a revelation for me, I thought; WHAT, now that's duplication at its best. You see what really happens for you as a speaker is when you speak you have an opportunity to sell products in the back of the room. Now for me the light went on, think about this just for a moment I first charge you six hundred dollars to come and speak at your venue for a couple of hours about my book. In the back of the room I have my books, CD's, DVD's and more for sale. After the two hours I have made $600 dollars for speaking and $4,000 for selling my products, do you see what I mean?

Now are you in the speaking business or are you in the selling your products business?

*Before you realize it, you're in control again*

# Chapter Three - Tools and Techniques

I want to give all of you who are either new to the internet world or new to the business world or both, a look at a few of the things that are absolutes when establishing a successful online presence. First you will need what's called a (Landing Page), ok, what's that, right? Imagine this, you contacting me and we have a conversation, I enjoy the conversation and so do you at the end of the conversation we both say bye and that's it. But let's say I want to contact you again but I can't because I have no way or doing it. A Landing Page will allow you to leave your email address and name and will send you an email requiring you to confirm me as someone who may contact you again. Second is an (Opt-in form) which is always on the landing page, that is where you actually insert your name and email address. Third you will need what's called an (Email Campaign) what that consists of is a series of brief messages that will go out to the people that have filled in the opt-in form that you have on your landing page. And the beauty of all that is it's done through what known as auto responders, which means that after you fill in the brief messages with what you want, once someone fills in the opt-in form they automatically within seconds receive an email to their address requiring them to confirm so that you may contact them without being considered as Spam. The (Auto Responder) is included in the email campaign. Fourth you will need a (Good Picture) of yourself to post. Fifth if you have (Testimonials) use them, if not begin working on getting some of those as soon as possible because they have a great impact on your viewers. Sixth and final is remember that ALL your marketing efforts should be generated toward your landing page, because once someone fills in the opt-in form your system actually takes over and does all the work from that point on.

Another angle that I wanted to inform the entrepreneur of was the mindset of staying motivated. If you have never started a business or ran a business there are things that will happen that will cause you to begin to question yourself and whether or not you are capable of actually doing it? Much of the opposition will come from people who are your family, friends, co-workers etc... And the list goes on and on. At the end of the day you will need to be able to look yourself in the mirror and say, I will see this through. Because without you it will never work. A few of the ways I recommend staying motivated is to: always pray to the God that you worship to, read people who are positive, forward thinking, and uplifting, and most of all don't allow the outside influences to take over your inner thoughts, processes, and decisions. The growth process for your business will without a doubt consists of three key areas that MUST be consistently growing and those are: First (Knowledge) it is absolutely necessary that you continue learning. Second is (Stay Focused and Positive) the world is full of noise and influences that will quickly and easily take you off course and will eventually cause you to stop all together. Third (Continue to take Action) there will be times when you will feel as if you are not going fast enough, there will be times when you will ask yourself if you are in the right business, or where's the money that you should be making, and the list goes on and on. One of the things you have to have is perseverance; it is imperative that you constantly fight through all the naysayers, financial obstacles, and any other situation that will occur. Which is another reason that my suggestion to all beginning entrepreneurs is to decide on the business you want based on your passion for what your are doing rather than the money, because once the money stops or if it never starts you will quickly change directions and choose to do something else, just for the money. Now let's discuss a few of the differences between a start up business of the past and a start up business of the present online. If we go only a short twenty years ago, you would need. 1. A Location. 2. A Product or Service3. Start up cash-(for monthly expenses) 4. Marketing and Advertising 5. Furniture for the location 6. Equipment 7. A drop shipper to send out your product 8. Employees

Today in 2011 all you need to start up a legitimate and reputable online business is: 1. A Computer 2. Working knowledge of the internet, that's it. In today's online business world the start up has changed significantly. For the price of a computer either desktop or laptop you have all that's necessary tools to begin your new opportunity. The playing field has never been more equal simply because all the things that you will need access to is available with only a click of your computer mouse. For instance the number one requirement of the past is location; today you can work from home hence the term home based. The number two requirement of the past product or service, today you are able to begin making real money selling someone else's product or service. The third requirement cash, you would need cash for electricity, water, material i.e. letters, staples, phone etc. Today you already pay your electric, water, phone etc, whether you have a business or not. Fourth is a budget to market and advertise your product or service, which in the past was either done on a daily, weekly, or monthly basis and without that no one would know that you were in business. Fifth you needed desk, chairs, rugs, pictures, and on and on to make your office look professional. Again, today all you need is your chair and your computer because no one is coming to your location, because you don't need one. The Sixth requirement of the past is equipment like: printers, phones, the machines that are actually producing your products and the list go on, and so does the expenses. Now the Seventh requirement is something that not everyone would need, but if you were making a product that needed to be delivered you did. But today when selling someone else's product they handle all of the shipping involved all you do is market the product online and that's it. The Eighth and final requirement of the past is the actual number of employees that you will need to run and operate your new business. Today everything needed to run and operate your online business can be done by you and only you. All the necessary tools to accomplish this are only a mouse click away. You can also reach hundreds and even thousands more people simply be signing up and marketing to certain online internet sites. And as you know, the game of business is reaching more people who are interested in what you have to offer. Online marketing is done simply by putting your product or service, or if you are in the beginning stages of you business, someone else's product or service in front of a possible client. Now it's very important to realize that unlike the way you would market in the past, today when marketing online you don't ask the possible client to purchase your product. I know that goes against everything that you have learned or have been taught about marketing, but in today's society you only want to give value in your first contact with your client. And the way you do that is again give something for FREE. This should be things like: a newsletter, an audio, an eBook, a CD, a DVD, and the list go on. Now if that goes against the grain for you, it's a must that you change your way of thinking. For in today's business blueprint when marketing online people don't want to be bombarded with buy this, buy that, and buy now. Let me give you this small example, if I am interested in learning the different types of phones that are available to purchase for my personal use, I don't want to see only one I want to see several, and learn about the different uses that are available for each phone. I will make my decision based on what I need the phone to do for my situation. And if I am bombarded with your phone over and over I will loose interest in what you have to offer very quickly. My word to the wise when marketing online is ALWAYS give value before you try to sell anything.

One of my favorite and easiest ways to understand something new is to follow the process. The process always has a step by step format. What I will do with you in this section is take you to a few places to set up your first blog. Next I want you to understand that a blog is a fantastic way to build communities and generate massive amounts of traffic. Another reason people choose not to get involved with something is because they have a tendency to think that everything is expensive, and they don't have any money. The truth is that there are literally hundreds of tools available to you online that are absolutely FREE. For example I'm am going to give you two places to go today and sign up, and within five minutes you can have your blog up and running and both are totally free, that's right I said free. The first site is: www.blogger.com and the other is www.wordpress.org. Once you have your blog set up you can then post daily to it in the form of text, audios, videos, pictures and other ways. The reason I enjoy blogs is you are able to include Links. Now there are a couple of types of links First there are paid links and then there are the type that most beginners love they are the free links. Keep your mindset focused on the fact that the major purpose of these things I am explaining to you today is to generate traffic. Now simply for your understanding, there are three types of traffic, the first doesn't cost you anything and its traffic through Face book, YouTube, or Blogs etc. Second is traffic through what's called performance traffic, the long and the short of that process is you generate traffic through affiliates. For example let's say you are paying your affiliate 40% of a sale, you are only paying your affiliate when he or she makes a sale. And that is what's called paid based on performance of traffic driven to the website.

Third is what's called paid traffic, what happens with paid traffic is you put money into an account and indicate how much you want your daily limit to be such as five, ten, or more dollars and when someone clicks on your ad to go to your site you pay a certain amount per click. There are several paid traffic programs but one of the most popular is Google AdWords. I indicated earlier that you can also purchase paid links and one of my favorite places for that is www.adbrite.com be sure and go there at your leisure and check out what they have to offer.

While I was learning the business of real estate, I would go to seminars, buy audios; I would even take other investors to lunch to pick their brains. After finally understanding what was actually happening I made a decision that I would become a Whole Sale Investor. When I began I had a partner and we started our own business and we were on our way. We would go to different neighborhoods and do what's known as (drive for dollars). We would look for properties online, we would put out signs, we would place ads in the paper, and we would use all the tools available to investors. And after about a year my partner decided she no longer wanted to be an investor, now at this point I had to make the decision to continue or go back to doing what I was doing. But reflecting on a quote that Robert Kiyosaki said: my goals had changed; I no longer want to work for people the rest of my life. So I continued and for another six months I struggled and finally I started to put properties under contract and make money. You see as a wholesaler your job is to find the property, put it under contract with the seller and sell the contract to another buyer. For doing that you are able to put in your fee to the new buyer and get paid at closing. It's very much like an affiliate in the internet marketing world because it's not your product you are making money from, it's your knowledge. Now after owning my own corporation for four years I was introduced to the world of online marketing, and fell in love with it. I have always been interested in home based businesses and now is a prime time to learn and apply what you've learned because of the economy. The odds of a person losing a job today is higher than every before simply because of the internet. With technology increasing the way it has things will only get worst for employees, which is one of my motivations for writing this book. I truly believe that even though you may have a job, and I think you should until you are able to maintain your lifestyle without working, it behooves everyone to do more than think about having something on the side that they are learning that will give them a second income stream. Many people who have lost their jobs have to learn a new skill, try and find another job in the same field or simply are unemployed. The alternative to that is to start your own business. For you to begin now as an entrepreneur is a little late, but not too late. Having said that many of you still have a job either fulltime or part time so my goal is to introduce to you the world of online marketing so that you not only continue learning, because the internet is so vast that the learning never stops but you can also set up alternate streams of income.

I am a person, who believes in multiple streams of income, and over the last twenty years I've probably had some twenty or more businesses, not all have made money but they have all taught me something. Once you have had success in the business world it's not easy to want to settle for the working lifestyle. And even if you do continue to work, position yourself to build you own business on the side in what ever you're interested in. Someone once told me that the answer is in the books, and it took me many years to really get that, but now I totally get it. In order for you to continue to grow you need to continue to learn because things change and it's a must that in order to stay in the game you have to stay informed. Today the way I learn, is as if I am going to teach, and that's exactly what I want to do is teach so it works very well for me. Now I wouldn't tell you this if it weren't true, once you start to learn and apply what you have learned, you to will begin to teach it to others as well, because the internet is a relationship building type of business. That's right in order for you to really become successful online you will build relationships with hundreds and even thousands of people. They will begin to move from what's called suspects, to prospects, and then to buyers or clients. Now as these relationships go through the funnel and begin to buy then you have the ability to continue marketing more and more products of value to them. The beauty of this process is it's all done from your home or where ever you choose and the cost is very minimal. But perhaps more valuable than the money is the fact that these systems are duplicatable, which means you not only can do the same thing over with another product but you can teach it to others as you own product. For instance once I finish writing this book I will be able to add CD's, DVD's, eBooks and more as part of my own product line.

One of my reasons for writing this book and doing everything I do is I really enjoy speaking. I'm also a motivational speaker and I love to speak to groups of people about things that I know about, because I am constantly telling people that people will pay you for what you know. And if you are doing anything in the business world once you start to grow, you will need to increase your speaking skills. That's the reason I have a website called www.speakwithlarry.com that teaches you to overcome your fear of public speaking. When I began speaking I was very nervous and I would sweat, that's right for about ten or fifteen minutes I would sweat. Now after that I was ok, and able to really enjoy the message I was delivering. So I joined Toast Masters and begin to speak every week and before I knew it I would still sweat but only for about five minutes, and in my mind that was growth. Today it's not a problem for me at all I simply want to be in front, and deliver the message and share some great information with people who want to hear it. Which is the direction I have set for my life, ok, let me give you the 411 on my plans it's late tonight and I am getting a little tired but I want to share this with you first, and I am going to make sure this gets in the book, if you ever see or hear me remember you read it in my book. I will speak at venues all over the country, I will have my own products available to purchase, and it will all be because of you.

One of the techniques I learned early in my online marketing career was to make sure that my marketing business was as duplicatable as possible. Along with always remember that the less I had to talk, the more my business was duplicatable. Now that may not make sense to you, but just think about this for a moment, if you had to duplicate something the less there was to do the easier it would be for you to accomplish it. My motivation for reaching out to as many people as I can is in part due to the actual opportunities that are available right now. Although millions of people have lost their jobs or have been downsized, they still have to some how continue. Continue doing what's necessary, living, dreaming, growing, just because we go through something as devastating as losing our jobs does not mean we give up. When you agree to open your mind and decide to start your new online business there will be a number of questions you will have, and that's alright you should have questions, however before you decide which MLM company you would like to be a part of there are three questions you should ask first. First, is this something I can do? Second, can I make money at it? Third, can you help me? Asking these three questions will allow you to determine whether this is a company you would like to join. If the answer to either of those questions is no, do not join. It has to be something that you can do, you have to be able to make money, and the person who brings you in or sponsors you must be willing to guide you until you actually understand. The main reason for that is you will sponsor others and you will need to guide them through the same process, which is the main reason for the system being duplicatable.

Writing articles is another simply wonderful way to market online especially if writing is really something that you enjoy. For me I never wanted to write, I actually began to write simply because you could write an article and post your photo and a link to your website or blog, for free. Now I'm not against paying for certain services but I want to teach my readers how to start and run their business with as little cash as possible. The first site I started writing for was www.ezinearticles. com and when you begin which I urge you to do, after you complete an article or two you will actually become a published writer and receive a small banner to place on your website or blog or any place you like. Writing not only benefits you through marketing, it also requires you to think more about things like titles, content, structure, and the list goes on. This is a way of allowing you to become more creative which is necessary in the growth of any system. After I had written ten articles my creative juices really began to kick in, and I wanted to write more and more and I truly believe you to will feel this way, simply because of the satisfaction that you receive after each successful publish. Now remember I said I didn't want to or at least had no desire to write, today I have over thirty five articles on three different sites. Wow, that's amazing to me. I'm going to give you a couple more sites that you can go to and sign up with and start to write your own articles. Another tip: always remember to put your photo and a link to your website, blog, or any place you want your readers to go on the bottom of your article in the correct position. www.goarticles.com and www.212articles.com .

The reason I wrote this book and made it so short was two-fold, first I will write other books, two more in this series. Next, with everything always moving so quickly I've found it to be more realistic for someone who may, or may not, be and avid reader to pick up a copy, start and possible even finish in a day or two. This being my first book I really wanted to make sure you received value that you can take and use today. This is a very basic but effective format for marketing yourself on different social media sites. First you want to position yourself as an expert, regardless of the field you select whether it's diet products, information products, or even auto products none of that matters. What matters is that you look knowledgeable and informative about that product. Remember your products responsibility is to solve a problem for the client, so they want to know that you know what you are marketing. Once you are looked at as someone who knows what he or she is doing people will get on board with you and start to value your opinion or suggestions. Next you will want to build your list and that's simply collecting email addresses and names. One of the beautiful benefits of the internet is once you have your system in place to receive those two things you actually open doors to other possibilities. You see the internet business is one of relationships, now you have sites where you have three thousand or five thousand friends or followers, while you probably don't know all those people personally think of it like this, Michael Jordan had millions of fans or followers and still does, Emmitt Smith has the most rushing yards in the history of football and has millions of fans or followers but neither of them knows all their fans and some friends on a personal level. However they still have influence on some of the decisions that those friends and fans make in regards to purchasing certain types of athletic wear. It works the same with marketing online, once you have established your brand and others begin to know you and your product as being one of value and integrity they will not only follow you but will also purchase your products. You have to remember that at the end of the day the person who's doing the buying is looking to solve a problem either for personal or other reasons.

Keywords are a topic I haven't covered yet but it's paramount for your success in the internet marketing game. What are keywords you ask, good question first you have to understand just a little about how the actual process works for your site to become on page one of the search engines. What happens is once you insert a word or phrase in the query box, the system begins, that's step one. Step two is the search engine has systems in place that looks for that specific word or phrase and brings those up in a order of relevancy, for instance if you type in (cars) it will take you to a page that has that word in the different key spots more often. Those key spots are: Title, Tags, Headlines, and the Body text. Also there are two types of keyword listings; the first is called Organic listing that's the type that's free to you. Next is Pay per Click listings which are pretty self explanatory you pay for those listings on a per click basis. Tip: when you are inserting keywords in those key areas don't over do it, I mean don't over stuff the keywords on the page try and write naturally and use a variation of target keywords like; plurals, synonyms and other words. When you are adding your keywords your ultimate goal is to rank high in the search engine ranking so one of the things you will want to find out is what the phrases are your potential customers are searching with. This actually refines and reduces the process because you will be able to use a narrower window to get the results you want. And example would be if you are in the flower business your potential clients would be searching for things like, roses, hanging plants, potting soil, etc... And not books, shoes, etc, get it. One of the most common mistakes when selling products and services online is not properly segmenting your market. For example let's say you are selling cars, now everyone needs to drive but not everyone has the same need. Families like the roominess of a mini van, where a single person likes the sexiness of a smaller perhaps more sporty type of car. The key to success when selling anything is to narrowly target all groups and speak directly to them. Now there are strategies involved in the success of keywords, that your site, or blog, or which avenue you choose to market within will need a hierarchy with a homepage and the keywords that your homepage will target. This is how it should look, the HOMEPAGE links to the CATEGORY PAGE which also has the keywords to target, and in turn it links to CONTENT PAGES these are sites like articles and videos which of course has their own keywords. FYI- it's always harder for new sites to compete with already established ones so look for keywords that offer higher popularity with little competition. Keep in mind that this is only the basis of a beginning strategy, and it's up to you to build it up. So monitor your traffic and sales of the individual niches in keywords produced, look for signs of success and build up on them. If a keyword is doing particularly well adding more content and link building will enhance the success and bring more traffic to the niche in general.

Ok, I touched earlier on links I want to expand on that topic just a bit more because these are intertwined with keywords in a way. There are two types of links internal and external both are used to get better search engine rankings. Now if getting to the top of page one on Google is something that appeals to you, and it should be, it's important to learn how to leverage internal linking text, of which you have complete control. While also understanding external links which you cannot control but can influence. Internal linking text comes in two different types , first is NAVIGATION MENU'S and next is BODY TEXT these are links you can use to link to other documents within your site. Remember to make your anchor text out of the keywords for which you want to be highly ranked, for example if you own James's shoes you can make it where when you run the curser over James's shoes the hand will come up signifying that this is a link and it will take the reader to another site. Now external links are what's known as inbound links what that means is they are arriving at your site from other websites. However since you are not the author of the site you don't have total control of the link. A couple of facts to ponder are 1. It takes time get to the top and 2. The Search Engine Optimization never stops, not even for the most developed websites. Now as you find new niches and keywords you have to keep creating new content pages that you optimize for them and attract relevant inbound links from other sites. Links are one of the preferred tools in the online marketing business because they are very simple to implement and they can be used in articles, videos, forums, and just about any place that you have text, a picture, or a method to receive a link. Once I had ordered business cards for a particular business that I had done the research on and decided I would become involved with. It was a home based business and required no upfront capital; I liked the product and was really excited about the opportunity. After about three months in I actually read the policies and procedures section along with the terms and conditions section as well. I couldn't believe what I was reading. It actually had in writing in black and white, that they could cancel my subscription at any time for no reason. It also stated that they had the right to take two of the first three people I brought in and place them on their down line, at the time I wasn't really familiar with what actually went on in a down line verses a up line, all I could see was the opportunity for big money because I have always been comfortable with recruiting people into an organization. Before long my instincts started to move me to think about whether I should be involved with this company or not. I guess the real eye opener came as I got to the bottom of the terms and conditions statement and found that this particular company had several complaints via the Better Business Bureau so needless to say I did get out but more importantly from that point on I always read the policy and procedures and terms and conditions section and so should you. Although we want to believe that people are for the most part good, it doesn't mean that systems are not in place to take advantage of the unsuspecting. I chalked that up as a lesson learned that I will definitely pass it on to others.

Throughout this book I will from time to time insert some very interesting facts about the internet and computers that will without a doubt enlighten you as well as educate you. Enjoy each of them and increase your knowledge base that will be very helpful in the future for you. For instance: *The first popular web browser was called Mosaic and was released in 1993.* What's important in life is being able to continually learn, and you do it whether it's learning things that you can use toward a better life, or learn things that keep you in the same position. Because lack of knowledge is very expensive. *Tim Berners-Lee in 1990 coined the phrase "World Wide Web" and is also considered by most people as the person who started the whole thing rolling.* These are only a few of the examples that are to come, and as you can see if nothing else they are lessons in themselves. Another direction I intend to take you the reader is to a place that allows you to go at your own pace. It's been my experience that if you are required to learn something that you don't really have an interest about, or something that requires more studying than you are use to, you have a tendency to loose interest. Which is why I have chosen to write this book in what I call an unorthodox way? Since the people who use the internet have such a varied range I wanted to reach the beginner, someone who not only is not computer literate but may or may not want to do all the reading necessary to understand because of the overwhelming amount of information. Also the individual who is on the computer regularly but for whatever the reason can't seem to generate any type of income, perhaps because of their lack of understanding of how to actually put everything together.

Many people, even though they may use the computer on a daily basis do not know how and why the internet started. So let me take this time to give you a little fact, *It all begin with time-sharing of IBM computers in the early 1960's at universities such as Dartmouth and Berkeley in the States. People would share the same computer for their computing tasks. The Internet also received help from Sputnik! Because after the Russian Satellite was launched in 1957, President Eisenhower formed*

*ARPA to advance computer networking and communication.* Since the start of those lean days of trial and error the internet has grown to a level of inclusion that not only has superseded any and all expectations, but has proven to become an avenue for start up business as well as many other opportunities. The time to put your thoughts and dreams to work has arrived, and the investment has never been lower, the knowledge you need to produce the results you want is literately at your finger tips. Another example of how effective and fast the internet has grown is, *it took 38 years for radio to reach 50 million users, which at that time was incredible. It took 13 years for TV to reach the same mark, and then along came the internet and after only a short 5 years it had reached that mark.* Amazing right, absolutely, no longer do you need to attend four years of college to receive the training needed to begin the business of your dreams and its all possible.

Now I want to give you a bit more incite into Larry James the person, I am the father of 2 children a son and a daughter. My son at the time of writing this book is 31 and my daughter is 24, both college graduated, and both married with children. My son has made me a grandfather 4 times and my daughter has 1 daughter. They are all joys in my life and I now understand what it means to have a linage to leave for generations to come, because my son has 3 sons. I love all my grand children the same, but the knowing that my name will continue to live on really makes me happy. Ok, from time to time I will insert other valuable information about the author along the way. Now back to the reason I am writing this book.

*Finally, experience the Full Benefits of Ownership*

# Chapter Four - Affiliate Marketing

*I made a few mistakes (on purpose) find them and go to CashfromSocialMedia.com for you new business opportunity.*

I would like to paint a picture of what you may look like when you make the decision to become a business owner online. Since you probably don't have a product to market your first and in my opinion the best option until you become more familiar with the online process is called, AFFILIATE MARKETING. What's that you are probably asking yourself well let me explain, this is the process of marketing someone else's product's or systems and receiving a commission for doing so. It doesn't require any of your own money and you are able to learn as you go. Many companies have a training format set up to teach beginning affiliates so that they are able to generate more money quicker. And more often than not you are able to receive commissions in the 40 to 60 percent range, and all you do is post links, or articles, or banners, or just a number of things that allow the customer to view and click on and purchase what's available and you have a sale. The number one reason I recommend this way of entering the online business is two-fold first it zero cash from you, and second it come with instructions from the company that guides you through the process, which as time goes on you will realize is invaluable. The quicker you catch on which is really easy to do, will spark your understanding and before long you will want to market other products and there is no limit to the number of products or systems that you can market. Once you start to receive a few commission checks you can at that point see the true benefit of being an affiliate. Now keep in mind that you will want to at some point create your own product because that's where you actually begin to move at a faster pace online and in other venues, such a speaking about your book, product, information and the like. And remember you are not only growing a company but you are growing within, and that's what makes the journey so great. I will keep emphasizing that the time has never ever been better than NOW so jump in and start.

As I indicated earlier I am also an advocate of great, inspirational, and motivational quotes so throughout this my first book I wanted to insert a few of my favorites.

*"Unless you are prepared to give up something valuable you will never be able to truly change at all, because you'll be forever in the control of things you can't give up."*— *Andy Law Creative Company*

*"Nothing is easier than saying words. Nothing is harder than living them day after day."*— *Arthur Gordon*

*"The greatest discovery of my generation is that human beings can alter their lives by altering their attitude of mind."*— *William JamesPsychologist*

*"Nothing can stop the man with the right mental attitude from achieving his goal; nothing on earth can help the man with the wrong mental attitude."*— *W. W. Ziege*

*"You can not always control circumstances, but you can control your own thoughts."*— *Charles Popplestown*

Those are just a few I would like for you to ponder and process, because as I said true growth involves growing from within first. And remember that only you know what you like or don't like no one else and when you decide to involve yourself in a business make it in line with what you truly like and enjoy, and you will never regret it.

We all go through situations and experiences in life no one is exempt for having a bad day, receiving bad new, or just not feeling physically up to par. And many times we question the reasoning involved, but some things are not for our understanding, however some things work the same way every time such as "seek and ye shall find", "give and ye shall receive", and my favorite "in order to get something you have to give up something". We often want to have the nice cars, homes, lifestyle but we are not willing to give up or make sacrifices to get them. We want to hold on to the same friends, the same bad habits, and even the same old out dated thoughts and information that we once had. In today's fast pace world one must be able to adapt to all types of situations both good and bad. As you live and experience life's day to day every now and again you will get what you would consider great news and want to share it with people that you consider your friends, and family. Often the response you receive won't be what you expected; now why would someone in your circle of friends or family not be excited about your success? Let me tell you, people for the most part want to be successful and live a comfortable life, but don't want to make the sacrifices necessary to achieve that standard of living, yet they still want it, and many times at the expense of someone else. So having said that, once you reach a certain level in life you MUST leave certain people behind. You have to in order to grow to the level that you want to grow. Because you are making the necessary changes to understand the processes. Now remember I said you are making the change, not your friends or family members and because of that, envy, jealously, and other types of negative things creep into the minds of those not changing. And if not on that level the longer you allow them to remain around you on some level the resentment will show up and most of the time it is at the very worst time, for example when you really need their support to accomplish a certain task or perform a specific job. And it's up to you to feel and watch for certain signs that let you know that you are possibly in danger of becoming exposed to such a situation. Now the saving grace in all of this is, one it makes you who you will eventually become, and two by weeding those personalities from your system will allow you to move at a faster pace toward your goals.

Now is a great time for me to go into GOALS, these will be absolutely necessary for your growth regardless of what you are doing. My suggestion is to maintain between three and five short term goals, short term being six months or less. And at least 2 long term goals, long term being three to five years. The way it works is as you accomplish one short term goal you add another and all should be in line with your long term goals. You will begin to feel powerful and responsible as you are completing your goals, and that satisfaction alone will keep you focused. If you are able to complete your goals really quickly, you need to make them loftier, because you should have to make certain concessions along the way and if you are able to go from goal to goal without much adjustments you simply need to step it up a little for example if you are a car salesman and your goal is to have five sales in thirty days, and you are able to have five sales in fifteen days you should increase your goal to nine or even ten sales for the month. Many people don't understand some of the other plus's that come with setting and reaching goals it also builds character and sparks something inside that make's you become more creative, and positive. After you have accomplished a certain number of successes in regards to reaching your goals others will begin to see another you, that will be the more driven and focused you, and they will want to become part of that new you, because everyone loves a winner. And that's exactly what you are slowly becoming. Now a final point about goals, these are personal to you and you alone. Remember to line your short term goals in the direction of your long term goals make the necessary adjustments as needed and press on.

Here are more of the fabulous quotes I want to share with you.

*"A leader's role is to raise people's aspirations for what they can become and to release their energies so they will try to get there."*— David Gergen

*"Reflection is looking in so you can look out with a broader, bigger, and more accurate perspective."*— Mick Ukleja and Robert Lorber

*"You must take personal responsibility. You cannot change the circumstances, the seasons, or the wind, but you can change yourself."*— Jim Rohn —

*"The first method for estimating the intelligence of a ruler is to look at the men he has around him."*— Niccolo Machiavelli

*"Education is the ability to listen to almost anything without losing your temper or your self-confidence."*— Robert Frost

*"Others inspire us, information feeds us, practice improves our performance, but we need quiet time to figure things out, to emerge with new discoveries, to unearth original answers."*—Ester Buchholz

*"If the people knew how hard I had to work to gain my mastery, it wouldn't seem wonderful at all."*— Michelangelo —

*"It's not the will to win that matters—everyone has that. It's the will to prepare to win that matters."*— Paul "Bear" Bryant

In my opinion, the world we live in has many geniuses, and they come in all sizes, shapes, colors, and have different levels of intellect which is a testament to the power and brilliance of our Lord. We ALL and I do mean ALL have something to both learn from others as well as teach others, knowing and understanding that, if you are alive today it is for a specific reason and not just a random act of luck or something intangible like that. Simply because you don't know or understand the reason is not a justification for you not to be the best you can be. Trust and have faith that the reason you are here is for the benefit of the whole, which was designed by our creator. I told you that I believe in the concept of building on the Mind, Body, and Spirit on a daily basis and when you are deciding on a way to increase you effectiveness in life whether its Financially, Intellectually, or from a giving perspective which is the Spiritual, all you need to do is trust that there's a power greater than yourself and NEVER believe that just because you can't see how something can be done by you doesn't mean that it can't.

Another point about the author that I will share with you is every time I began a new venture, regardless of how small or large the opportunity. I always look at it from the perspective of learning something for the first time. The reason that I view it that way is I want to truly know it well enough to teach it. That's very important to me because I understand that the process is more valuable than the end result or the prize if you will. When you look back on how things have gone in your life if you simply pause, or slow your mind down long enough to remember, when you learned to ride a bike. Can you remember the many times you fell, got up and hopped back on and went a little farther it was a process with the end result being you having the independence to ride when you wanted, or perhaps because you simply wanted to ride farther, maybe you wanted to learn to do tricks on the bike like ride with no hands, regardless of what your determination to learn to ride was, today all you know is the end result. That's right all you do is get on and ride, you very seldom fall and you have no fear of riding because you learned the process, which means when you have children do you think you could teach them how to ride a bike? It works the exact same with starting a new business, there will be fear, there will be things to learn, and yes you will fall, you simply have to get back up, hop back on and ride. Just keep in mind that once you are able to master the business that you selected the payoff is excessive. You no longer have to work for anyone else, ever. You are able to enjoy the true pleasures of living life on your terms, which may include spending more time with your family, taking vacations to places that you once only dreamed about, and from the spiritual perspective I talked about earlier being able to help a larger number of people, or giving back. This is one thing that I believe we would all do if we were given the opportunity.

Here we will discuss a few of the things to be mindful of when going through the learning process. First I want to say I know it won't be easy, and really nothing worth having is ever easy. Next it will be important for you to line things up as you go to accomplish small tasks and began to have success early. Third when I am teaching, my message is to never focus on only the money. Fourth be very aware of who is on your team, and understand that certain members that are on your team will probably not be with you when you reach your point of success. Fifth and the final concern for this section are outside influences. Now let's take a more detailed look at the five concerns, Number one, there is a quote that says the more money you have in business the less knowledge you need but if you don't have money the more knowledge you need. In other words you have to bring something to the table, and if you have neither knowledge nor money your journey will be more learning intensive, because the learning part is very low cost. Number Two, as you start to set up your goals list don't make goals that you won't be able to realistically reach in the time you allot. For example if you are marketing a product online and your last three months you have sold a average of four per month don't set your next months goal at nine or ten, it puts you in a position to having a let down when you don't reach that goal or even worst you may begin to loose interest all together. Number three, when you focus on just the cash that you are making as soon as the cash stops so does your interest in what you are doing. That is almost all ways the way, which is why I never recommend you join a group or business simply for the money, what I do suggest is that you find out what you passion is and work on building a business around that. Number four, I have witnessed many people who have a great idea for a business and start out, before long they either get a partner or employees, or both which is great and the way it should be because business is a team system. Now at some point after monitoring the growth or lack there of, certain decisions must be made in order to correct any bottle necks, or stopping points in the system. That correction may require you to terminate someone that you have known for some time or perhaps a family member if that's the situation, you have to be able to make that correction and go on, period. Because your success or failure depends on it. Ok, Number five, this should be your easiest to correct but more often than not it's the most difficult to correct. We all have ego's and there will be people who have the ability to get under our skin by saying things like, it will never work, you have tried things like that before, you can't do that. And if you start to listen to that noise it can easily lead you to thinking they may be right or start you to doubt yourself. You can't allow that line of thinking, what you need to do is simply stay focused on the process and the result, because the process will handle the day to day and the result will handle the naysayers. Before you know it the very same people who are talking the loudest about you not succeeding are the same ones who want and need your input or information.

It has been my experience that in order for me to stay motivated about either learning something or teaching something is the ability to share things with others so here are more great quotes for you to pass on, and remember sometimes when you tell people a quote it make you look a certain way in their sight.

*"Nothing is as embarrassing as watching someone do something that you said could not be done."— Sam Ewing*

*"Life is a succession of lessons which must be lived to be understood."— Ralph Waldo Emerson*

*"Life is like a library owned by the author. In it are a few books which he wrote himself, but most of them were written for him. "—Harry Emerson Fosdick*

*"The great blessings of mankind are within us and within our reach; but we shut our eyes, and like people in the dark, we fall foul upon the very thing we search for, without finding it."—Seneca(7 B.C. - 65 A.D.)*

*"Nothing will ever be attempted if all possible objections must first be overcome." —Samuel Johnson*

*"The only way of finding the limits of the possible is by going beyond them into the impossible." —Arthur C. Clarke*

*"Courage is doing what you're afraid to do. There can be no courage unless you're scared."*— Eddie RickenbackerWorld War I hero

*"One learns peoples through the heart, not the eyes or the intellect."*— Mark Twain

*"In the course of history, there comes a time when humanity is called to shift to a new level of consciousness, to reach a higher moral ground. A time when we have to shed our fear and give hope to each other. That time is now."*—Wangari MaathaiLecture upon receiving the 2004 Nobel Peace Prize

*"What we see depends mainly on what we look for."*— John Lubbock

# Chapter Five - Adjusting who you are and your focus.

This section is specifically inserted to reach who you are, from the inside out. There will be a number of reasons why you will want to learn the type of business opportunity that I am presenting here. Perhaps it's because of the ability to work from home, or maybe it's something that you have always wanted to do but was afraid. Trust in the fact that a major factor involved in your choosing not to do it, or choosing to do it will be in large part to your self esteem. Many times when we get a opportunity to invest in something that requires our own effort and creativity we have a tendency to evaluate how we feel and more often than not choose to listen to our self talk, saying things like, you can't learn all that's necessary to run a business, or I don't have the time to do that. Regardless of what's being said negatively it all comes from the smallness in you, and that's directly from your self esteem. Now again you may be asking why I am putting this in my book, its simple, I want to introduce you to a different way of viewing yourself; studies show that two out of three people have low self esteem. This more than we realize places us in a state of not allowing us to pursue what you enjoy or is actually meant for us. We are all individuals and if I were to ask you to look within yourself and tell me what you would really like to be doing as a way of life your answer would be different than mine and probably most of the people you know. The majority of people who are working for a living are not working in the field that they would choose if you ask them what they would like to be doing. The reasons for that are many folds but just imagine for a moment you actually running you own business online, can you do it, should you do it, and will you do it. Only you can answer that, however I will tell you this, it's 2011 and if you think that computers are going to go away, you are sadly mistaken. Every day there's more things added to what's available for you to do online which make our lives easier and able to go at a faster pace. It's almost like a television show we used to watch growing up called the Jetsons, they had the ability to move from place to place at a very fast pace. So it's going to become vital that you start to learn something about computers as quickly as possible. Now speaking just a little more on self esteem this is something that you need it's not something that you simply want. It's also something that only you can give yourself, so start to believe in yourself and live your life with standards and morals. One of my favorite quotes go like this; *"Never let what's MOST important to you become a slave to what's LEAST important you, and what's most important is how you feel about yourself and what's least important is how others feel about you."* The first time I heard that was from a guy named Stephen Pierce but I'm not sure if it's his quote but I felt it would help with your decision to allow you to feel good about yourself.

There are also some of you who have always said that I don't want a business I would rather work for someone else. As you know that way of thinking is all but outdated today, even if you are working at a full time job many times it simply doesn't pay enough to allow you to live a comfortable life.

Today's time's requires everyone to become more creative as well as do things that they normally wouldn't entertain. When I first learned the business world and how it really works many things surprised me including, how easy it is to start the business and how difficult it is to maintain as well as grow the business. One basic reason for that for me was at the time not having a mentor to follow and be evaluated by. Today there's all type of mentors for just about anything; the problem is no longer finding a mentor but selecting one who has your best interest in mind. I will be the first to say that yes, there are people online who have another agenda. The more you become familiar with what's going on; on the net, you will be able to quiet the noise. What does that mean? It means once you start to do things on line you will start to receive opportunities, information and that's just the beginning. The good news is shortly after you begin, things will become crystal clear that there are a lot of things going on there. You just can't focus on everything being sent your way, and you will need to be selective in who actually takes up your time. Remember you are going to start to read more than you have in possibly the last ten, fifteen, or even twenty years. Which is the main reason I am keeping my books short, quick, and to the point? One thing I know about learning something new is if it's a book, and it's too thick most of you won't read it. And that will also cause you to lose interest because you are either intimidated or just no longer interested in learning because you anticipate more and more of the same. If you are somewhat familiar with the computer, things will naturally be easier for you and many times when that's the case you will become a leader for someone else. Always remember to give back when ever possible, it's called planting seeds and karma. Planting seeds because the internet is a people business and when you start the first contact you have with your possible clients will not be to sell them something. Now remember from earlier chapters that the process of generating cash online is just a little different from other businesses. You first need to share information or products in order to build a relationship with your possible clients, that's all done very easily with email, or links, or other creative ways to make contact. As you're learning marketing online you will discover that there are several ways to do the same thing, many are necessary and some are not.

However when you learn the way through the first time, then you can learn the second, or third way later. I am bringing this information in this format to you for the first time in an effort to get you to understand better how the universe works in accordance with PLANTING A SEED, NURTURING A SEED, and HARVESTING A SEED. I am going to write a series of three books that will guide you through the entire process. Success at anything requires a process and you probable won't be real good at it at first, and if you are good, you can get better. In this first book I will assist you in the planting of the seed part, which is very important when it comes to getting the results you want. One reason is you want to make sure you are only planting one type of seed. If you notice when a farmer plants his crops he only plants one type of seed for each section of the field. He doesn't plant corn, beans, and peas in the same section of the field. A couple of reasons for this is they all have to be nurtured differently, another is the growth process would cause them to become entangled with one another which would cause their growth to be stunted or maybe non existent. That very same process works in your mind when planting thoughts that you want to one day in the future harvest. My suggestion at this point for you would be, to decide that if you want something better for yourself and your family and believe that you deserve something better then understand the process and begin the process. There will be many things involved in the planting process that will feel uncomfortable to you at first and that's simply because of the shift in weekly, daily, and even hourly thoughts that will begin to enter into your mind. You must understand as well as realize that as you begin to read more and see more you will begin to want more. The doors will actually begin to open for you in many different ways and at many different times. It's actually a journey of momentum, for with each day of growing comes more confidence, and assuredness in the fact that you have indeed made the correct decision and that the end result can be exactly what you both want and expect. So to recap quickly the necessary thoughts involved in this process is to first plant only one seed per field in your thoughts. Not that you can't have other fields that you are planting and plan to harvest and you should, because you have the ability to do many things from a mental perspective at once. However the point to remember is that all the fields require different types of nurturing, and not to confuse them. Also important to note is that many times the life you live or the circumstances that you are faced with on a daily basis can cause you to have thoughts that take you away from the seed that you have planted which will eventually cause that seed to die. So it's very important that you stay focused and fight through your external situations because if you don't, they will begin to become your reality. And at that point it not only becomes difficult for you to remain focused on the seed but actually takes you away from even believing that it's possible for you to have the result of the harvest.

Now shifting to another perspective that you will be confronted with and YES, I said WILL, be confronted with is what we call outside influences. These outside influences can be deal breakers; they have the ability to make you turn your entire focus in another direction at the drop of a hat. And what are these influences: your job, your friends, your money or lack of, your family, and the list goes on and on. You see once you make a decision to change something about yourself that goes against what has been what we will call the norm, it causes a chain reaction. This chain reaction is not only felt within, but it also effects the external, meaning your time will need to be adjusted, your availability will no longer be whenever is ok. People who look at you in a certain way will begin to look at you differently. Things will start to be said about you that has never been said before. Mary is always on her computer, I think she has a problem, she is never around us any more and on and on. Understand the reason you are no longer available is what's happening within you is you are being taken to another place intellectually which will take you to another place financially and you are not only willing to go, but are eager to go. Let me ask you a question, have you ever seen or experienced something that was really spectacular or beautiful and said to yourself either verbally or mentally WOW, I wish so and so were here to see this? At that very moment there was a shift in reality, for you knew that it was not possible for that person to be there. And if you ever tried to explain what you saw and what you felt you could never give it the proper explanation because it was a moment in time where you had to be there to get it. That's what happens to some people when you make the decision to do something that they don't understand, they are never able to see what you see therefore can't and won't really be on board with your journey. Which in actuality works out best for you because not everyone is meant to take the journey with you and the quicker you can eliminate the one's not meant to travel with you the better. The only problem with that is most of the time you are not able to see that and you continually want that person or persons to be with you and can't understand why they can't go. You have to be able to make a decision based on what's best for the whole, if you see the people who you are so insistent on coming along are not contributing, or are weighing down the growth you must dismiss them and move on. There's no other way. Remember the question I asked earlier about seeing something that you wished someone else could see? If they can't see what you see it's not necessarily their fault they simply haven't been exposed to or experienced the shift or change necessary for them to move in another direction. And remember this, most people will never give you permission to do what they can't or won't give themselves permission to do.

The next angle I want you to view your decision from is one of a poverty mindset. That's right, POVERTY do you realize the number of people who live their lives day in and day out viewing it from the mindset of there not being enough. As incredible as it may seem many people go through life just getting by, simply because someone who they value that persons opinion has said to them this will never happen or that will never happen and they actually go through their entire lives not trying new and different things. I ask you is that insane or what?

In my studies I have found that some people take advice from people who have never read about how to do a certain thing or even tried to do that certain thing, as being the truth. This only makes you a slave to continue in the path of the past. Let me give you an example, I have worked at a job for over thirty years combined the year is 2010 and there are still people who get their check handed to them, WHAT!! Rather that payroll deduction. Their reasons vary from I don't trust computers, to I like having my money in my hand, again, WHAT!! Come on people if those are the reasons you don't want payroll deduction that's not really the reason, the real reason is someone has told you that they don't trust computers and they like having their money in their hands and you signed up for that way of thinking and have not shifted that way of thinking. Of all the people who work in my location probably 85% have payroll deduction and you have never heard of anyone's check being displaced or not deposited what is it not to trust, when you can get yours in your hand and either lose it or simply have to go through the process of going to the bank to have it either cashed or deposited. Maybe it's just me or maybe not. Either way one of the reasons I attribute that way of thinking to no growth or slow growth is it's not your own, you must be able to evaluate the information available and make a decision on what's best for you and your system, and no everything is not for everyone so if you are simply looking to maintain rather than grow perhaps moving at a faster pace is not what you want. However the take away I would like for you to get from this segment is, it's vital that you are able to adjust and adapt to new things and new ideas, and not focus on information that was given to you by someone perhaps years ago that has become outdated.

This will be the final series of quotes that I will leave with you hopefully you have enjoyed them thus far and maybe you've even shared a few. The main reason I am leaving these is two fold first when you repeat them to others you will look intelligent, and second when you repeat enough of them you will be intelligent.

*"Fear is a natural reaction to moving closer to the truth."*—*Pema Chodron*

*"Life shrinks or expands in proportion to one's courage."* —*Anais Nin*

*"Every submission to our fear enlarges its domain."*—*Samuel Johnson*

*"Fears are hurts that roost in the nest of our memory."*—Robert Schuller

*"Ultimately we know deeply that on the other side of every fear lies a freedom."*—Marilyn Ferguson

*"When we blame, we give up our ability to change."*—Steve Straus

*"The brain is more slowly stirred by the ear than the eye."*—Voltaire

*"Of all the things you wear, your expression is the most noticeable."* — Confucius

*"To make oneself understood to people, one must first speak to their eyes."*—Napoleon

*"The face is the mirror of the mind, and eyes without speaking confess the secrets of the heart."*—Saint Jerome

In today's fast pace world which is ever changing we seldom get the opportunity to truly make a decision and follow through with it, I employ you to reach within who you really are and do something that you have either always wanted to do or something that you feel you have to do. Now is the time and this is the place. Tip: as you are going through your learning process reflect back on this book and re-read some of these quotes and keep your head in the game, and remember this is the planting of the seed, not the nurturing, or the harvest, those are to come.

Ok, that's it, the rest is up to you. I want you to know that I believe in you and one day I would like to meet you and introduce myself. Where ever you a right now is not a reflection on where you can be. A word I would like to plant in your mind right now is CONSISTANCY this word makes winners out of losers, it makes believers out of skeptics, and it delivers the exact result that you want. Everyone starts in the very same place and that's in their mind. Once you decide to incorporate the action to your dream you will begin to feel a certain amount of adrenaline, at that point focus on exactly what that feels like and never lose that momentum until you have reached the point that you are able to do what you do in your sleep. How long should that take, that all depends on you. Everyone's resources are different, as well as their determination, remember you can't make money and excuses at the same time.

Another of my personal goals before I started to take the time to write this book was and still is to become a professional motivational speaker. Which is why I love quotes and passing on great information to others. After following other speakers and finally being able to position myself to get speaking engagements it really increased my drive for that goal. Today I am speaking regularly to different organizations and the logical next step is to have a product to market, hence this, my first book. Understand that from the position of learning, two years ago I never would have thought that today I would be writing a book and through hard work and constantly moving forward I can now visually realize my dream of being a motivational speaker. And not just a speaker but a businessman who markets his and others products both in public and online. For someone who has been employed for the government for the last thirty plus years to transition from something that has allowed him to comfortably raise his children, and prepare to retire from that profession to do what he loves is nothing short of a testament to hard work, mistakes, focus, learning, more mistakes, preparation, determination, more mistakes, and finally the result I wanted. I do want to say that many times when you are trying to get your system up and running the way you plan, a thing called life will meet you head on and cause you to slow down just a little. Some times in the guise of you either having to spend more time with the family, your hours change at work, or perhaps you need to start to pick up the kids from school or athletic events. When you are doing what you both enjoy and want to do you will eventually get back to it somehow. Sometimes it takes only weeks but other times it may be a year or two for you to actually restart the engine in your machine, and get back in the drivers seat. However since it's a part of you, it never really leaves your thoughts and you always have plans to get back to it. One of the people I study is named Baeth Davis, and she says if you want to have success just finish what you start, sounds simple right, well in theory it sounds simple but to actually complete everything you start would be extremely difficult to do. So you have to choose your battles carefully and adjust when necessary, the only downside to that is many times the adjustments may take literally your whole life. A great example of what I mean is my own life's work, but more recent and relevant is when I began to write this book. My initial goal was to simply create a product to market, after about ten thousand words my mindset began to change and the project began to become more personal. Now at this point I realized that writing a book meant more than just creating a product, and my respect for authors and writers of all types has changed in a way that I will never look at them the same. The project has gone smoother than I thought and many times it's because you don't really know everything that's actually taking place, and again sometimes that's good. But as I said, I have worked for another company pretty much all my life, and now in the latter years of my life because of persistency, focus, and hard work I am seeing my dream become my reality. Yes I said MY reality, and you have to do the same.

One of the comments I like to tell people is that: I believe that everyone has a book within, and probably more than one. Now after starting the process involved with this book I am sure of it. The reason I am saying this is in order for you to expose yourself to the type of success that you really want, will require you to give up something. Today I am working full time, I have a online book store, I am making videos, writing articles, I have two websites that market my speaking business which is called Speakwithlarry.com, I am an affiliate marketer for several companies, and I'm now I'm writing this book, plus I work fulltime. With all that I still had to give up something and for me that was my time, because it takes time to do all those things. First you have to remember that I am learning while doing or OJT- on the job training-, but the desire that I have to finish what I start, when it comes to my goals are very important to me and should be to you as well. The main reason I have been able to accomplish the things that I have is because of the access to easy learning. Yes easy, and the fact is its pretty much free learning also. Because computers are almost everywhere now and everything you need to know is accessible with only a mouse click. That's why for you to become more computer literate is not an option, it's a must. One of the ways I recommend to assist you in gaining more familiarity with computers is to join one of the social media sites; facebook.com, twitter.com, and linkedin.com are just a few. And as a personal note: please get your mind away from thinking that doing things online is not safe. I hear story after story from people who don't want to learn anything about computers use that as an excuse. And all that really does is poison the mind of others who would like to learn but are reluctant to because of that statement. It's also amazing to me that some people don't want their own business of some type, but everything isn't for everyone, and having said that if you are one of those people who really don't want your own business when someone comes to you and says they would like to have their own business, encourage them and point them in a direction that will benefit their dream if you can.

I would like to ask you if you know the number one reason people choose not to attempt their dream. If you said FEAR you are absolutely correct. If fear is the number one reason people don't attempt their dream, then any little thing that is said to them negatively will deter them even more. Now through my studies and living life I will tell you that more often than not we give certain people far too much control over our lives and our thoughts. I indicated earlier that everything isn't for everyone and if you choose to put your faith and understanding in someone who falls in that category you potentially put your dreams in jeopardy. Now insert all the intangibles necessary to have your dream, lack of money, lack of correct knowledge, lack of time, and that list increases believe me, what do you do? Well if you're like many, you stay where you're comfortable or where what you call safe. Ok, I'll give you twenty, thirty, or even forty years ago the term job security had meaning, today it's not the same. If you are one of the unfortunate people who lost their jobs in the last couple of years then you can probably relate to the struggle involved when your stream of income not only slows but stops. Looking back if you had a part time business that you had begun six months or even a year earlier you could simply increase the time you were doing it and increased your income. Another reason people choose not to go for their dream of having their own business is they can't see themselves doing it. In other words they don't have the confidence in themselves. And that's truly unfortunate because a lot of time it's because of things that happened early in childhood that makes a person choose to hold themselves back. The fact that there are several ways to deal with the childhood, conditioning to redirect ones energy, effort, and so on is available in many cases. The point here is that we all have things that we deal with on a regular basis, so it eventually becomes our responsibility to take one hundred percent responsibility for our decisions. And blame only ourselves for mistakes, fear, or lack of confidence that we have. And remember that there are both internal and external influences that affect our path in the direction we choose to go. So just because things didn't go perfectly in childhood or what ever the reason does not eliminate anyone from reaching inside and moving on. Because when it's all said and done the final decision is still up to you, and only you.

This is information that will benefit you when preparing to select a company to work with online. Now if you are already working with different companies online this is a great way to check and see whether your company measures up. And remember a company may have the best products and a great pay plan, but if it's lacking in some of these ways you could lose everything, in the blink of an eye. First does the Compensation Plan pay part-timers? Fact: 95% of networkers are part timers? So make sure that people can make a decent income working a few hours per week. Beware of companies that advertise how many millionaires they have created. Make sure it's not at the expense of those "at the bottom". Everyone should be able to benefit. Take the Compensation plan test-Ask yourself this question: "How many people do I need on my Team to earn a recurring income check of $500 per month?" This number varies but keep in mind that there are companies that require as many as 400 and then there are others who require 50. Remember it's not unusual to see well-established companies that require 150 to 350 people, but what's amazing about that is they are still able to attract new distributors. Another point you should consider is if your upline can't or won't answer that question, you should RUN. If you are making 5% to 8% commissions on a product, you are being extremely underpaid. If a company stresses "Recruit, Recruit, Recruit", you should "Run, Run, Run!" Keep in mind that the purpose of any business is moving product from the company to the end-consumer. The majority of your commissions MUST come from product sales: otherwise it wears the suit of a SCAM. And finally if you work a plan that does not pay on product volume, somewhere in the process you will lose money! But more importantly, you will lose credibility too.

Many of the things that I've learned about online marketing I was introduced to through a system called Mentoringforfree.com. It has invaluable information and all for free, a few of the other things I want to share with you about their system is, if the product would not sell without the business opportunity attached it is ILLEGAL. If you can't pay with a credit card and must pay by cash or money order it's ILLEGAL. If the distributors collect the money while the company stays at arm's length, it's ILLEGAL. If you must have a Retail Merchant's account, the company is SCAMMING YOU. The reason I am telling you this is when introduced to something new people have a tendency to go back to what they normally do or what feels comfortable, or safe. But that's not for you, you are armed with information that will steer you in a direction that is full of companies that are reputable and stand behind their products, and their people. Now remember it is still up to you to take full responsibility for learning the Skill Set necessary to accomplish the result you seek. Keep in mind that this is your business and you will want to take understanding the process very seriously. Now much of the things I've covered you may or may not already know, but try and understand that this business is a lot of fun, and as you increase your knowledge about how everything is done you will agree. My final word to you about starting your new online business is: If you don't see the system working for you right away, don't try to reinvent the wheel. Remember you have to plant the seed, nurture the seed, and then harvest the seed. The time that you spend learning over the next six months, ten months, and even a year from now will GUARANTEE that you WILL become fully functional with your online business. You will have to always give up something to get something. Try and see what the world is really offering you and everyone else which is an opportunity to no longer be dependent on a job that you really don't like or doesn't meet your financial qualification.

I would like to take this time to personally thank you for purchasing this my first book; it's been both a learning and growing experience for me. And the same type of commitment it took for me to write this book is the same type of commitment it's going to take from you to get from where you are now to where you would like to be in the future. I mean really the choice is TOTALLY yours and think about how fast time goes, and it's the only resource you can't get back once it has passed. All I am trying to say is life is not a trial run it's one time and that's it, what you don't do this time you won't get to do. My wish for you today is that you are able to see the possibilities within yourself learn and act on your experiences and always continue to grow to the level of success that only you consider satisfactory. Again I want to warn you that we only get one chance at life, and to repeat a quote that I once read about doing what you love only for money, **you never hear a man on his death bed asking for more money**. I truly hope you receive that in the spirit it was meant because time is all we have and it is limited, and for everyone it will end one day. Don't allow others or your inner self doubt to dictate your future, take full control and responsibility for you and the results of your life. That's right, after finishing this book no longer except being in control of only ninety, eighty, or even seventy percent of your life, take one hundred percent control, and except responsibility for your mistakes learn from them and move on. Don't continue to live your life as if there will always be a tomorrow, start to live your life as if there is only today. May the Lord bless you and yours,

www.ingramcontent.com/pod-product-compliance
Lightning Source LLC
Chambersburg PA
CBHW051212050326
40689CB00008B/1284